Molested

One Mother's Shocking Discovery

By Audrey Doomer

Recognizing Evil Series

Why You Should Read This Book

Our lives begin to end the day we become silent about things that matter -- Martin Luther King

When my children were growing up, I believed they were safe. I trusted my husband with them, because he appeared to be a good father. But I wasn't seeing reality. What I saw was a carefully crafted illusion - one that lasted for years.

I'm sharing my story to show that supposedly well-informed parents can be blissfully unaware that sexual abuse is happening to their child. Because I spoke to my daughter about sexual abuse, and told her to tell me (or "Daddy") if someone ever gave her a bad touch, I believed she would tell me. But parents cannot solely depend on children traumatized by a molester to disclose abuse. Sexually abused children live in fear - fear of their abuser, and fear of the consequences for disclosing abuse. Non-offending parents need to know just how devious child molesters are, especially the ones known as "Daddy."

If you're a parent, this book is for you. In these few pages, I tell the story of my daughter's sexual abuse disclosure, describe missed clues, and give insight into how child molesters deceive. My story is raw, and personal, and I wrote it with the intention of opening eyes.

No one wants to believe child sexual abuse could be happening in their family. I didn't think it was a possibility, either. By the time my eyes were opened, my little girl had endured years of massive pain and suffering. Don't let the same thing happen to your child.

This story is absolutely true. Names and identifying information have been changed to protect the innocent.

Table of Contents

Chapter One

Chapter Two

Chapter Three

Chapter Four

Chapter Five

Chapter Six

Chapter Seven

Chapter Eight

Chapter Nine

Chapter Ten

Chapter Eleven

Chapter Twelve

Chapter Thirteen

Chapter Fourteen

Chapter Fifteen

Chapter Sixteen

Questions and/or Comments?

Chapter One
Blissfully Unaware

I had to force myself to not dance out of the courtroom. *A thousand bucks a month for the next ten years! This is what it must feel like to win the lottery, or at least the Publisher's Clearing House Sweepstakes.* I feel giddy at the thought of this bump to my bank account, courtesy of my soon-to-be-ex-husband. On the way back to work, I let loose and dance in my car to the rhythm of the bass and drums blaring through my car speakers. It is a beautiful day.

Two months before, I separated from my husband, and took out a restraining order against him. It was hard to believe we had reached this point. He was my first everything - first kiss, first and only person with whom I'd shared a bed. I wanted to be married one time, and one time only, but I was drowning in his constant jealousy, insults and thoughtless behavior. I stayed with him for our children's sake, knowing he was an awful husband, but believing he was a good father.

The horrendous marriage had produced two beautiful, sweet children - Mya, the oldest, was quiet, obedient, and quick to help wherever she saw a need. She was also the smallest girl in her class. James was a bit hard-headed, and always wanted to do things his way. Case in point - He refused to go to first grade when the new school year began; instead, he ran to his former teacher in the kindergarten room and insisted he was going back to her. I had to promise him the astronomical amount of $10 to get him to walk into the first grade classroom.

Despite my painful marriage, I didn't want my family to be broken. I thought my children needed their father, so I stayed with Jason. Naively, I believed divorce was wrong unless I had proof he cheated on me - one more time. I had forgiven his prior indiscretions after he pleaded with me to stay with him. But the thought of another eight years of wedded torture was incomprehensible, and I told him if he wanted a girlfriend - no problem. We could divorce and he could start another life with someone else. I knew what was in store for any woman attaching herself to this man, and I wanted my freedom.

I had no clue that the daily phone call hang ups I received were the key to collapse his reign of pain over me. Jason adamantly denied knowing the caller, but I was thrilled to find the phone number in his address book, which was normally hidden in his car. When I pointed out the number, he responded by slamming me into the bathroom wall. "Call 911," popped into my head, and I listened. The police showed up in less than five minutes, arrested him for domestic violence, and deposited him into the county jail.

Never again would I be subjected to Jason's crazy-making. No more tap dancing on clouds to keep him happy. No more accidentally crushing eggshells with my feet, and apologizing profusely because he insisted I was being disrespectful to him. During the past two months, I had gotten used to the fact that I was a single mom of two young children, and the upcoming child support gave me strength that I could raise my babies alone. Jason traveled a lot due to his job, so custody of the children was never an issue.

Since the separation, thoughts of homelessness tormented me, but today - today everything is different. In a couple of days, I'll get my first child support check, and it will cover almost two house payments. I couldn't understand why he refused to pay the mortgage; even though divorce is imminent, our children still need a place to live, and I can't afford the mortgage by myself. Didn't he care about his children?

But a thousand extra dollars a month means I don't need to worry about finances. Jason and I will split child care costs, and I'll be able to take care of Mya and James. Maybe even splurge on takeout once a month or more. Life as a single mom is looking fantastic, and I was looking forward to it with financial support.

Back at work, coworkers peer at me with raised eyebrows as I study dull spreadsheets with a smile. Time accelerates, compressing hours of a usually dull, monotonous job into a few, brief minutes filled with unbridled joy. After work, I pick up my daughter from the after school center, then head toward the sitter's house to get my son. My cheeks hurt from hours of smiling. Life couldn't get any better.

I had no way of knowing that on this day, my drive to the babysitter's house would be anything but routine. This is the day that split my life in two; before the awakening, and after. Nothing would ever be the same again.

Chapter Two
Unspeakable Disclosure

Mya waits in the car while I knock on the babysitter's door. Ms. Chris is silent as she opens it a few seconds later, her expression serious. I'm a little concerned, as this kind, gentle woman usually greets me with a smile and "How are you?" A quick look around proves my rambunctious son, James, is still in one piece. *Whatever it is that's upsetting her, it can't be that bad.* "Hi, Ms. Chris. How's everyth – "

"Audrey, I have to tell you something. I'm so upset. I had to take a Valium a few hours ago to calm myself down." *Valium? I think it's time for a new sitter.* "I've got some bad news. Really bad news." Her hands shake as she wipes away a tear.

What could be so bad? "Ms. Chris, what is it? What happened? Did James get hurt?"

Ms. Chris looks at me, her face creased with concern. "Mandy told me that James said Mya puts his pee-pee in her mouth."

Her words sting my mind with the ferociousness of a thousand angry wasps. I shake my head to delete the awful picture from my mind. "I'm sorry – I didn't hear what you said. Please repeat that."

"Mandy told me that James said Mya puts his pee-pee in her mouth." Stunned, I'm speechless for a few seconds as I struggle to process this information.

I shake my head again. "No. There's got to be a misunderstanding somewhere. Mya wouldn't do that!" I zoom into the living room, balancing on my high heels. Smoothing my skirt, I kneel down next to James. He looks up at me, still holding toy trucks in his hands. "James, Ms. Chris just told me something about you and Mya... Is it true that she puts your pee-pee in her mouth?"

My five-year old son breaks eye contact with me and looks at the floor. The corners of his mouth angle down. His bottom lip protrudes and trembles. He nods his head, and looks up at me with huge blue eyes, eyes too big for his face.

Forcing myself to remain calm, I ask, "How many times did she do this, James?"

"Two times - in the bathtub."

She's eight years old! How can she know anything about oral sex? "She shouldn't be doing that to you, sweetie. Come on, let's go talk to her." James grabs my outstretched hand, and we walk to the car in silence. *It has to be someone at her school. When she's not at school, she's with me or her father. I'm going to press charges against the pervert that would do this to my baby. Who could do such a thing to an innocent child?*

James and I hop in the car and buckle up. I turn to my tiny daughter and say, "Mya, James said that you put his pee-pee in your mouth." I pause for a few seconds, and then say, "Where did you learn to do that?"

My little girl's face turns to stone, and she twists away from me. She stares at the glove compartment. Her shoulders move up, then down, in a nonchalant shrug.

What? Why would she react to my question like this? Something's wrong. Really wrong. "Mya...has someone been making you do that?"

My baby girl turns to me and scrunches her delicate, sweet face. Her painful, agonized cry pours out – "Daddy! Daddy's been making me do that!"

I feel electrocuted with shock. I can't breathe. A loud, wailing sound of unrelenting pain fills the car. It emanates from Mya and me. The harsh dissonant notes lance the festering, raw wound in my little girl's heart. The secrets, lies, and despicable acts crushing her innocence are exposed at last, ready to drain.

Chapter Three
Shattered Illusions

At home, in the living room, I kneel down in front of my sweet child and hold her. Between sobs, I say, "Baby, I'm so sorry this happened. Mommy didn't know Daddy was doing that to you – I didn't know." Holding her cleft chin, I look into her beautiful, trusting eyes. "I'm so sorry." She reacts to my tearful apology with a hug.

Desperate for reassurance that it happened once, and no more, I ask, "Mya, Daddy didn't make you do that a lot, did he? It was one time, right?"

Her eyes brim with tears. "Mom, he made me do it *a lot*." Her words are relentless as they pound my brain.

That scum bag's done this more than once? "When did he start making you do that? Since we moved into this house?"

She shook her head. "No, since we lived in the two-story apartment. It happened the same day you went back to work."

Stunned, I say, "The two-story apartment? The townhouse? *Four* years ago?"

Mya nods. "Yes, the townhouse. He made me watch a videotape of people doing stuff and made me do the same thing." I knew what videotape she was talking about because he tried to make me watch it with him, and I refused.

"Doing stuff?" *God, please, I can't take any more.* "What else did he make you do?"

In a matter-of-fact tone, with maturity far beyond her eight years, she said, "He tried to put his front private part in my front private part and in my back private part. I told him he was hurting me, but he told me he didn't care and to shut up and be still."

I'm unable to speak for several seconds, and Mya points to the couch and loveseat. "He made me do it on them, on my bed, and on your bed. He would put KY jelly on me and Vaseline on his front private. He made me take showers with him and he would put his finger inside my front private, too. He also put his tongue in the middle of my front private."

I stare at my little girl, eyes wide open, astounded to hear words such as these come out of her mouth. *Her childhood has been filled with rape! Her innocence was stolen right from under my nose. I thought I was protecting her from the monsters in society, not knowing the monster was in my own home, sharing my bed.* I collapse as fresh tears flood my face and sobs of devastation commandeer my body. *God, help me! What kind of creature did I marry?*

Mya wraps her tiny arms around me again. For several minutes, I hold on to her, flabbergasted at the horrible reality of the situation. "I'm so sorry, baby. He will never, ever hurt you again. I promise you that. You don't need to be afraid of him anymore." *My baby girl is revealing the most horrific abuse, yet she's comforting me.*

"I didn't like him giving me a bad touch all the time."

"All the time? What do you mean 'all the time'?"

"It happened every time you weren't with us – when you were at work, or shopping, or at rehearsal. He would ask me if I 'wanted some.'"

This phrase was quite familiar to me, as Jason constantly harassed me for sex asking if I "wanted some." He often asked me this in front of our children, and it never dawned on me that either one of them understood what he was saying. This sick man was telling his own daughter every time he wanted sex with her mother, asking his daughter for sex, and raping her!

"Baby, why didn't you tell me what he was doing? Why didn't you ask to come with me to rehearsal or shopping?" *Why didn't I see what was going on? How could I have been so blind?*

"I couldn't tell you, Mommy. He said he would beat me really, really bad if I told anyone. He also said he would do something to put you in jail, and he would take me and James far away so we would never see you again. And he told me to stay when you went out - he said it softly so you couldn't hear." *Not only did he rape her for years, that piece of garbage burdened her with keeping his filthy secrets. He forced a little child to suffer to "protect" her family. What kind of sick animal could do this? God, wake me up from this nightmare.*

"No, baby. He lied to you. You're safe now. He will never touch you again. He's not going to take you and

James anywhere, and I haven't done anything wrong for the police to put me in jail."

Reassured that nothing would happen to us, she reveals another secret. "Mom? Remember the nightmares I have? I couldn't tell you about them because they were about Daddy hurting me." For years, Mya occasionally awakened me in the middle of the night, terrified, and crawled into my bed, where she slept peacefully. She always told me she couldn't remember the nightmares. For half her life, she had endured severe, repeated trauma at the hands of her "Daddy." Once she disclosed the abuse, her nightmares stopped.

Mine would soon begin.

Chapter Four
Reviewing the Reality

Mya and James go to bed early that night, and I contemplate the future. I know Jason is a coward, and I'm certain he'll flee the country once he finds out I know he's a child molester. Once he's out of the country, he won't send any money to help take care of Mya and James. How am I going to take of my babies when my income can't cover the mortgage? Will we be forced to live in a women's shelter?

For a few brief seconds, I contemplated making a deal with him. I considered telling him I wouldn't report him so he could stay in the United States and pay child support. But he would NEVER have visitation - ever again.

But what kind of message would that send to Mya? Would it make her believe that money is more important than reporting the horrible, unspeakable felony crimes against her? No. I can't NOT report him. There is no price that can be placed on my child. Reporting Jason is the right thing to do. Besides that - he can't be trusted. Not at all.

I pick up the phone and call the psychologist who had been counseling me as I dealt with the breakup of my marriage. "Dr. Smith, I need to bring my daughter to see you as soon as possible."

"Your *daughter*?"

Between sobs, I say, "Jason's been molesting her for years. I just found out because she molested her brother, James, and he told a little girl at the babysitter's, and the little girl told the babysitter. Mya told me Jason's been making her do the same thing, and she described all kinds of despicable acts that he's been doing to her. Is it possible she's confused? I believe someone's been making her do this, but I never thought it possible that Jason would do this to his own daughter! I thought he was an excellent father!" I wipe my nose and sniffle. "I don't know what to do. Can you see her soon?"

"I can see her tomorrow. Can you bring her in at 3:00?"

"Yes. We'll be there. Thank you."

I lie in bed all night, eyes closed, mind reeling. The cognitive dissonance makes it impossible to sleep. How do I reconcile my former belief that my husband is an amazing, wonderful father with my daughter's disclosure? I feel completely numb. Nothing is as it seems. The world I know is shattered, and the pieces embed themselves in my brain. I want to go back to the world where my little girl isn't raped by her father, but cherished, valued, protected, and loved. But that world is not reality.

Scenes from Mya's life repeat in a non-stop loop in my mind, and I view everything from a new perspective. From the moment of her birth, Jason "showed" me he was a good, responsible father, and that he loved her. Why would I suspect him of raping his own child? How could I suspect something so vile, so despicable, so *insane*, when he appeared to be a normal father? A child molester father wouldn't be so kind and so loving toward his daughter, would he?

Jason was with me during labor and delivery when Mya was born. He cried tears of joy, and doted on her. Was he crying because he finally had his own victim to groom from birth and rape at will? He didn't hesitate to change her diapers, prepare formula, or give her a bath. He seemed thoroughly pleased to have a child. I loved the way he would squat down to look her in the eyes when he spoke to her. I thought it was so special - a sign of his willingness to be on her level, and proof of their closeness.

As she grew older, he called her his "little princess," and always held her hand in public. He painted her room pink, and bought a pink and white comforter to match. She was "Daddy's girl." In the past, I felt my daughter was so fortunate to have a father that showed her how special she was, but now I see that he was rewarding her for being compliant and keeping his filthy secret.

We did the things normal families did together - we went grocery shopping, to the mall, to movies, to restaurants, watched tv together - how was I supposed to know of his secret, deviant life? Mya, James, and I went to church each week, and when Jason was home, he went with us. I listened intently to sermons discussing the sanctity of marriage with the theme "what God has joined together, let no man put asunder," not knowing I was married to a devil in human form. God definitely didn't put us together.

Because of my beliefs, I enrolled Mya in a Christian school. I wanted to ensure she was in a safe environment learning about God. Jason wasn't an active Christian, but he was raised in the church, and didn't object to her attending this private school. I thought we both wanted what was best for Mya.

Jason's sales job often took him away from home for one to two weeks at a time. I felt like a single parent during his absence, having to work full-time, take care of the house, and squeeze in my left-over time with Mya and James. The last year or so of the marriage, I noticed Mya and James having a decided lack of enthusiasm when I told them "Daddy's coming home tomorrow!" and asked Jason to try to find a job where he didn't have to travel so much. I was concerned that Jason, Mya, and James wouldn't have a close relationship unless he was home more. Fortunately, Jason was gone 80% of the time; the little time he was home, he caused the most damage he possibly could.

When he wasn't traveling for work, he acted like a homemaker and kept James with him. I would drop Mya off at school on the way to work, and he'd pick her up to eliminate after-school care charges. I'd come home to a clean house, food, kids bathed and ready for bed, and no dirty laundry. My heart melted seeing him kneel by the bed to pray with Mya and James every night. It never occurred to me that just a few hours before, he was raping her on that same bed.

During the years I stayed home as a full-time mom, I relished the chance to run errands by myself, not knowing what was in store for Mya when I did. Often, he'd take the kids to a pizza place geared toward children, where they'd stay for hours. It was a reward for being still while he raped her. When I got home, I'd find Mya and Jason curled up on the couch, reading a storybook together, or watching cartoons. It was the picture of perfect father-daughter love. Mya pretended everything was fine, just as he did. She had to follow the lead of an insane man. I trusted his "love" for his children, and he knew it. I never thought to assign an ulterior motive to anything Jason did.

I had taken out a restraining order against Jason two months before at the recommendation of the police. Jason wasn't permitted to come to the house or call, but was given visitation rights to the kids. We met in a neutral, public location for drop-off and pickup to avoid problems. Jason was scheduled for visitation twice, but only took the kids once. After that one visitation, Mya came back home dressed in inappropriate clothing that revealed her midriff, back, and most of her legs. I was stunned, as she had never worn such clothing before. Why would he buy clothing like this for her?

For the second visitation, he didn't show up, and didn't bother to inform me he wasn't able to get the kids. At this time, I had no idea what he was, and wanted to keep him involved in their lives. Jason and I were getting divorced; he wasn't divorcing his children. I was fully enmeshed in the lie that Jason was a wonderful father, and wanted to ensure his relationship with his children continued to be "good." I wasn't interested in using my children as a weapon against Jason - I had heard and read about women being vindictive like this and damaging their children for life, and I didn't want to do this to my children.

As I continued reviewing past events through new eyes, I realized why he was so generous on Mya's birthday - it was for three reasons: to make a lasting impression on his friends, to prove his wonderful father qualities, and to reinforce Mya's silence. Never before had he been so extravagant; he gave two huge lawn and leaf bags packed with presents to one of his friends who worked at the school Mya attended. Just a few months before, when he lived with us, Jason refused to replace Mya's too-small church shoes, saying he didn't have the money. But as soon as we separated, and he had three expensive attorneys on retainer - then he could afford large bags stuffed with toys? He also gave her a photo of himself taken by a professional photographer. I thought the excessive amount of gifts was quite strange at the time, but the motivation behind his generosity was now clear. Jason knew the woman he gave the bags to would spread the news of his birthday gifts to Mya far and wide, cementing people's opinions of him as a caring father, and Mya would quietly accept the gifts. Jason had perfected the art of manipulating everyone around him, and making himself appear to be a wonderful person.

Now I finally understood why Jason wanted me to work outside the home. When I was a stay-at-home-mom, he didn't have access to Mya like he wanted. When I had a paying job, he had many hours of unsupervised time with her. I had to drop my college classes and return to work when James was four years old because Jason and I had temporarily separated. During this time, I was impressed by Jason's dedication to his children - he picked up Mya from school, and got James from the babysitter's so I could come straight home from work. Only it wasn't for my benefit, but for his - he got Mya so he could molest her. James never saw anything because

Jason made him take a nap or watch tv while he did the unthinkable to his own flesh and blood.

I believed Jason would always love and care for his children, even if we weren't together. But child molesters aren't capable of love. Jason is a demon in a human suit, and continued access to Mya was all he wanted.

I married a monster.

Chapter Five
Documenting

After a long, restless night of no sleep, I get out of bed the next morning and call my employer. My request for several days off to take care of my daughter is granted. I worry about finances, because I have no vacation time. The mortgage has been unpaid since Jason left, and I didn't know how long we can live in the house until we are forced to leave. I won't be able to pay the remaining bills with a dock in my pay, but I can't function. Work and sleep are impossible at this time. I can think of nothing but the pain my daughter has grown up with, the evil thing I called husband, and how the world I had been living in was nothing but a fantasy.

Mya continues to tell me more disgusting things about Jason, describing how he grabbed her genitals at every opportunity, even when Mya and James were riding in his car. Jason would put James in the back seat to keep him out of the way, and every time Mya got in the car with him, he grabbed her genitals and held on to them. He did the same to me in the car when both kids were in the back seat. My protests were ignored. He treated us all as property to use and abuse.

At 3:00 pm, we see Dr. Smith for an evaluation and Mya opens up to her right away. It was surreal listening to my daughter again describe the disgusting, revolting things Jason did to her. Horror movies couldn't touch this. At the end of the session, Dr. Smith contacts the Child and Family Services Department and reports the abuse.

The Department of Children and Families, and the Sheriff's Department visit the house a couple of days later to investigate. The detectives tell me they will eventually need to speak to Jason, but will continue to gather evidence beforehand. Several weeks later, the detective assigned to the case asks if I would be willing to speak to Jason on the phone and record the conversation. The idea is to prompt Jason to say something incriminating. The detective also wants Mya to speak to Jason on the phone.

The thought of talking to him again infuriates me, and I am afraid of Mya being further damaged by any interaction with him. At our third session, Dr. Smith asks Mya how she would feel speaking to Jason on the phone, and I am flabbergasted as Mya begins crawling around on the floor, making baby sounds, and crawls into my lap, then Dr. Smith's lap. She regresses to an infantile stage mentally and stays there for several minutes.

After this session, Dr. Smith takes me aside. "The only reason she is not insane is due to you. You treated her like a normal child and provided the stability she needed." Years later, I understood how fragile my daughter's mental and emotional state was when I met a social worker, trained to detect abuse of all kinds, whose own child had been severely molested. Her daughter was institutionalized at six years old because her mind "snapped." This trained social worker had never detected the sexual abuse, which included being forced to watch her father have sex with with his own mother, the child's grandmother, multiple times.

Dr. Smith's report to the detective investigating Mya's case follows:

Dear Detective Jones,

This letter is a summary of my initial evaluation of Mya Doomer, an 8-year-old Hispanic female seen on 04/29/1997. She was also seen for follow-up counseling on 05/06/97, 05/20/97, and 05/27/97 at my office located at 123 Main Street. Mrs. Doomer requested that this writer evaluate her daughter's statements first made to her on 04/28/97, regarding sexual abuse allegedly perpetrated by Mya's father, Jason Doomer, and provide psychological treatment as needed.

TESTS AND PROCEDURES ADMINISTERED

1. Clinical interview with Audrey Doomer
2. Clinical interview/observations of Mya Doomer
3. Follow-up Family Psychotherapy

HISTORY AND BACKGROUND INFORMATION

History and background information was made available by Audrey Doomer. According to Mrs. Doomer, she was informed by her babysitter on 04/28/1997 that while James (5 years of age) was at his babysitter's house on 04/28/1997, he made a statement that Mya made him put his "pee-pee" in her mouth. When Mrs. Doomer asked Mya about the statement that her brother made, she reportedly stated that her father had made her do the same thing.

Mya currently lives with her mother in her own home. Her mother is employed as a bookkeeper. Her father, who is not a citizen of the U.S., but of Austria, works as a salesman for an international company. Mrs. Doomer has been seen by this writer since 02/25/1997 in individual psychotherapy in order to assist her in the process of coping with the break-up of her marriage following a recent incident of domestic violence. They are in the process of divorcing. Mr. Doomer has not been living in the home since February, 1997. Mya currently attends Lincoln Academy and is in second grade. According to her mother, she is a good student and presents with no academic or behavioral problems.

Mya does not present with any history of psychiatric illness or behavior problems. There is no family psychiatric history of mental illness or psychiatric treatment, with the exception that Mya's father has abused alcohol, received substance abuse treatment, and was imprisoned for DUI manslaughter. According to Mrs. Doomer, her husband continues to drink. A maternal grandfather also abused alcohol heavily. Mrs. Doomer denied any current or previous abuse of alcohol or drugs. Prior to this evaluation, she reported that her husband often forced her to have vaginal sex.

MENTAL STATUS AND BEHAVIORAL OBSERVATIONS

Mya was initially seen in this examiner's office on 04/29/1997. She arrived promptly and was accompanied by her mother, who remained in the room during the initial evaluation. Her mother remained silent during the interview, and Mya answered questions posed by this writer without coaching from her mother. Mya presents as a Hispanic female who appears her chronological age. She presented as friendly and courteous throughout the initial evaluation. During the interview, which involved an assessment of sexual abuse, she responded to questions directly, with steady, appropriate eye contact. She did not appear fidgety or hyperactive. The only point at which she refused to respond to questions and became tearful was when she was asked regarding any sexual abuse that she might have perpetrated against her brother. Her speech was of appropriate volume, rate, tone, prosody, and grammatically correct. Mya did not present with any psychotic features, such as auditory/visual hallucinations, delusions, obsessive thoughts or compulsions. There was no clinical evidence or unusual or bizarre thought content in her speech and there was no evidence of a formal thought disorder. Her affect appeared largely within normal limits except when she appeared sad when asked about any inappropriate touch between her and her brother. When asked how she felt, she said "happy" because now the abuse would not happen again because she told about it. There is no evidence of appetite or sleep disturbance. She presented with no anxiety when separated from her mother briefly.

Clinical Interview:

Mya was able to describe her current living situation well. She appears to be of average intelligence and was able to articulate her thoughts well. It is the opinion of this writer that her interview is a valid representation of her current mental status and experience.

A review of good touch and bad touch was conducted. Mya presented as being aware of what was a good or appropriate touch, and a bad inappropriate touch. When asked if she had ever received a "bad touch," she reported that her "Daddy" had given her such a touch. When asked where she was touched, she reported in her "front private" and "back private," pointing to her vagina and bottom. When asked what happened, Mya described that her father would take his "front private part" and try to put his front private in her front private and back private. She also reported that he put his front private in her mouth. When asked when this happened, she stated that it first began four years ago when she and her family lived in a town house. Her mother stated that four years ago they did live in a town house. She was unable to respond to questions regarding frequency, but described that this took place when her mother would go shopping or was out of the house. When asked where this would take place, she reported in her parents' bedroom. She denied that anyone else, including James, was present during any incidents. When asked what his private front part looked like, she stated that it looked like darker skin and motioned approximately 7 inches long. She denied that anything had ever come out of it. Mya stated that her father would threaten her with physical punishment if she disclosed to anyone this activity. She also described that he would tell her that she could go to "Chuck E. Cheese" if she did what she was told and did not tell anyone.

Mya denied any sexual abuse by any other adult or child. After this interview, a telephone call was made by this writer, with Mya and her mother present, to the

Child and Family Services Department. The mother requested that this writer make the call. This writer made the report to Gladys, identification number 005.

The following three counseling sessions included Mya, her mother, and brother, James. During the first session, no issues of sexual abuse were discussed with the children present. During the second sessions, the children discussed what situations made them feel certain ways. When the feeling "mad" was discussed, Mya spontaneously stated that she felt this way when her Daddy would spank her and give her a "bad touch." When the feeling, "afraid" was discussed, Mya spontaneously stated that she felt afraid the "first time" that her father gave her a bad touch. During the third session, after discussing how she would feel speaking on the telephone with her father that evening, she appeared to regress significantly, seeking to be held by her mother and this writer, crawling on the floor, making baby sounds such as "goo-goo" and pretending to cry.

CONCLUSION AND RECOMMENDATIONS:

In conclusion, Mya Doomer is an 8-year-old Hispanic female who is currently living with her mother, Audrey Doomer, and her brother, James. She has no history of mental health treatment or mental health problems. Mya reports that her father sexually abused her for years consisting of vaginal, anal, and oral sex. She described that he would "try" vaginal and anal sex, which may suggest no penetration during these occasions and therefore no medical evidence of sexual abuse. Given the fact that the alleged sexual abuse was originally disclosed as a result of Mya's brother, James, who described to his babysitter that his sister had sexually abused him, the evidence is strong regarding the likelihood of sexual abuse. Furthermore, Mya is a bright and articulate 8-year-old who responded clearly and coherently to all questions with the exception of the topic of inappropriate touch between her and her brother. She is highly credible in her presentation. This initial evaluation appears to be a valid estimate of Mya's mental status and experience.

Based on this evaluation, the following recommendation is provided. It is recommended that Mya participate in Family and Individual Therapy in order to address issues of sexual abuse and appropriate healthy relationships with caregivers and her brother.

This writer spoke with you on the telephone on 05/21/1997 and suggested that the perpetrator be held for a judge to determine bond due to concerns regarding absconding and retribution. It was made known to this writer on 05/20/1997 by Audrey Doomer that Mr. Doomer at one time stated that he would send someone to kill his wife if she caused him a significant degree of stress. Furthermore, given that he is not a citizen, it would be easy for him to abscond and return to Austria.

DIAGNOSES:

Axis I: Sexual Abuse of Child – V61.21

Axis II: Diagnosis Deferred – 799.9

Axis III: None reported

Axis IV: Moderate to severe stress, exposure to sexual abuse by father

Axis V: GAF = 60

It is a pleasure working with Mya. If you have any questions concerning this letter, please feel free to contact my office at 555-1212.

~~~

Mya's Global Assessment of Functioning (GAF) score was high at 60 (a higher score means less symptoms of psychological, social, and occupational dysfunction). I believe her score was high because Jason and I had been separated for 2 1/2 months when the abuse was disclosed. He had only had 1 visitation with her and James, and didn't have the opportunity to rape her because he was living with a friend at the time. Consequently, her stress levels were significantly less.

Several months into treatment, I asked Dr. Smith what kind of person could rape his own child. She replied, "A psychopath. Jason is a psychopath." I had never known this term could apply to him. I used to think psychopaths were crazed killers murdering people for fun. I had no idea psychopaths masqueraded as kind, loving people, and could pass for normal. If someone looks and behaves strangely, we know to keep our distance. But evil often hides under a veneer of goodness. Discovering that Jason is a psychopath started me on the journey to learning more about this personality disorder. What I found astounded me.

Dr. Robert Hare, one of the foremost researchers on psychopaths, developed a psychopathy checklist for mental health professionals to use when diagnosing psychopathy. As I read through it, I saw that Jason met the criteria in every category on the checklist. Even if he had not molested Mya, the problem in our "marriage" was not all my fault, as Jason repeatedly insisted, but was mostly due to his abnormal personality disorder. Psychopathy is a mental illness that has no cure. There's no way to make psychopaths safe to be around. Everyone needs to be educated on the subject of personality disorders, particularly psychopathy, narcissism, and borderline personality disorder. We must learn to identify people with these dysfunctions, and by understanding how they work, we can limit our involvement with them. Everywhere people with severe personality disorders go, they leave a path of pain and destruction.

I believe Jason has a few different paraphilias (a sexual desire or behavior that involves another person's psychological distress, injury, or death, or a desire for sexual behaviors involving unwilling persons or persons unable to give legal consent). Besides being a pedophile, Jason appears to be sadomasochistic.

Chapter Six
The Confrontation

The investigation was ongoing for several weeks while evidence was collected. Mya had to speak to the sheriff's department, the Child and Family Services Department, and psychiatrists working for the state. Her testimony with the psychiatrist was videotaped, and she had to demonstrate what Jason did to her with anatomically-correct dolls. Her medical examination was normal, or inconclusive for sexual abuse, just as 96.3% of all children referred for a sexual abuse exam:

http://www.ncbi.nlm.nih.gov/pubmed/12201160)

Jason had not penetrated her with his penis, but with his fingers, tongue, and Chap Stick. He was attempting to slowly enlarge her vagina using the Chap Stick container as a dilator. When Mya told me Jason put the Chap Stick container in her vagina, I remembered how patient, calm, and methodical Jason could be in situations that would make most people frustrated. One evening I was attempting to assemble a toy, but got upset because the pieces didn't fit together. He took over the project, and gently made the pieces fit. He handed it to me and said, "See? Don't force it. You have to be patient." He applied this same diabolical method of raping his child with a Chap Stick container, intending to penetrate her with his penis in the future.

The day came when the detective investigating Mya's case dropped off phone recording equipment for me to use when speaking to Jason. I paged him, and he called me within minutes. The conversation was supposed to get him to incriminate himself, but I was too angry and upset to think clearly.

The last time I spoke to Jason on the phone, before I found out about the abuse, I had a moment of weakness. Wanting to preserve our family unit, I asked Jason if he wanted to go to marriage counseling. I didn't know that one of Jason's friends was listening to our conversation on another phone line. He wanted someone to listen as I spoke in a pleading voice. Unfortunately, during this phone conversation I asked about reconciling. Months later, one of Jason's friends called me in the middle of the night to taunt me and tell me I was a liar, and that he was listening on the phone when I tried to get back together with Jason.

Now that I knew what Jason was, my attitude toward him was the polar opposite of the last time we spoke. I paged him, and he called me promptly. Shaking with anger, I said, "Jason, Mya's nightmares are getting worse. I need to find out why she's having so many nightmares and what she's having nightmares about. Every time I ask her, she says she can't remember. I'm going to take her to a psychiatrist, and you need to pay for half of the cost." He asked to speak to Mya, and I handed her the phone.

"Mya, Mommy says you're having nightmares. What are your nightmares about?" (When I listened to this conversation on cassette tape a week later, I was struck by how hypnotic his voice seemed; how he appeared to be simultaneously pretending to not know the reason Mya was having nightmares, yet his tone served as a warning for Mya to keep quiet about the abuse. The duplicity was truly crazy-making.)

"I don't remember." (Mya's sweet, innocent voice assured Jason she was keeping his secret.)

"Are you sure you can't tell Daddy?" (Great pretense and concern for her well-being, when all he was concerned about was himself.)

"I don't remember." (Jason was reassured of Mya's continued compliance in keeping his secret.)

Mya handed the phone to me, and I spoke into it, telling Jason coldly, "You'll be getting a bill soon, so look for it." I disconnected the line, and Mya and I hugged for several minutes. She was so brave, and I told her how proud I was of her. By the tender sage of eight, she had already dealt with situations that would make adults lose their mind.

The detective picked up the recording equipment a few days later and mailed me a recording of the conversation. Nothing in the conversation could be used against Jason. Maybe we would have handled it better if our interaction had been online, but at that time, very few homes had computers.

Before the detectives interviewed Jason in person, Mya needed to speak to the Assistant State Attorney's Office. By this time, she had grown tired of telling her story. For half her life, she had kept Jason's sick secret. She no longer wanted to speak to complete strangers about the disgusting things done to her by her "Daddy." Three years earlier, I taught Mya to sign the letters of the American Sign Language alphabet.

In front of the Assistant State Attorney, Mya began slowly spelling out her responses to the Attorney's questions using the sign language letters. The Attorney told me she couldn't take Mya in a courtroom spelling words like this. In front of Mya, she said that the charges would be dropped if Mya didn't tell her what happened. Mya clamped her mouth shut, and refused to speak of the abuse again. She wanted to move beyond it, and the thought of discussing it in court with Jason looking on was too much. She wanted it to end. I couldn't force my child to speak about the abuse again, and traumatize her further.

The last step in the investigation was soon to take place - interviewing Jason. I knew he would flee the country as soon as he found about the investigation and told the State Attorney's office. They said nothing could be done about it, but I decided to speak to the State Department of Law Enforcement for another opinion.

On my lunch hour, I spoke to an agent in person, saying, "My soon-to-be ex-husband has been molesting my daughter for years, but there's no medical evidence. My daughter talked to the Sheriff's Department, the Child and Family Services Department, psychologists, and psychiatrists, and they all believe her. But now she refuses to talk to the State Attorney's office, and they have no choice but to drop the charges. I'm afraid he's going to flee the country and get away with it. Can you confiscate his passport or do something to prevent him from taking off?"

The agent said, "No, ma'am. Just be glad he's leaving. We don't need people like that living here."

I was beside myself. Locking Jason up wouldn't erase what happened to Mya, but allowing him to flee the country without experiencing any consequences was wrong on so many levels. He deserves to be locked up for the rest of his life, away from society. Little girls aren't safe around him, and neither are women. All the people investigating the case believe Mya, but her refusal to speak to the State Attorney's Office prevented them from moving forward with the charges.

A couple of weeks later, the detectives went to Jason's place of employment before he arrived. When he checked in with the office, he was directed to go to the room where the detectives waited. They introduced themselves, and asked him to sign a "Consent to Interview" form. After he signed it, they said, "We are here because your daughter, Mya Doomer, has made allegations of sexual abuse against you."

As soon as Jason heard this, he said, "I want a lawyer."

Without Mya's willingness to speak to the State Attorney's office, and with the lack of medical evidence, the detectives couldn't hold him. But he didn't know this. Instead, like all guilty people, he ran. He ran when no one was chasing him. Jason resigned from his job that very day, emptied his bank and retirement accounts, turned in his expensive car, booked flights for his girlfriend and himself, and fled the United States two days later.

Jason never experienced any legal consequences for raping his own daughter. Four years of the most heinous, disgusting, sick, against-nature crimes, and he was freely allowed to leave the country. He paid me a total of $700 in child support before the detectives confronted him. Once he left the country, he never paid another dime. I had to collect public assistance for years while I pursued my degrees. The state tried to locate Jason for reimbursement of this money, but couldn't.

Jason's home country does not have a child support reciprocity agreement with the United States. For me to collect child support, I would have to retain an Austrian attorney for thousands of dollars. I don't have thousands of dollars to spend on an attorney. Through the grapevine, I've heard he has a very well-paying, international job, and can easily afford child support. Jason got away with a capital felony, and financially abandoned his children, to boot. In this day and age of global connectivity, all countries should enforce court-ordered child support owed in other countries.

Chapter Seven
The Aftermath

Unbelievably, Jason had one more weapon in his pain-causing arsenal, one he had prepared for his exit strategy in case he got caught, and he used it well. Apparently, he anticipated what to do in case he ever got caught. Causing severe emotional pain and distress to another is icing on the cake for psychopaths. Jason knew that I have the emotions and feelings of a normal person, unlike him. He also knew I would give my life for my children, and that I truly believed I did everything possible to keep them safe.

Before leaving the United States, Jason used a technique frequently used by psychopaths and other disordered people. Jason's preemptive strike was to invert the truth, which gave him power and control over the perceptions of everyone who heard his version of events. He told his friends I was angry he had a girlfriend, and made up lies about him, saying he molested Mya. Because no one believes Jason capable of committing such a horrendous crime, people feel tremendous **sympathy** for him. This is one of the hallmarks of a psychopath - they try to get people to feel sorry for them. If you meet someone who elicits your sympathy - beware. Once someone expresses emotions of sympathy and caring, the psychopath knows he/she can easily manipulate the person. When psychopaths fool someone, they experience a powerful sense of "duping delight." This makes them feel superior. I can't even begin to imagine how superior Jason feels knowing hundreds of people believe he's innocent of child molestation.

The news spread like wildfire all over the country. People everywhere believed I had spitefully lied about Jason, accusing him of child sexual abuse. People from church, from the Christian school Mya attended, and my mother's friends - all of them heard the news. In their eyes, Jason is an innocent man forced to leave the United States due to a vindictive, hateful wife. They still give me dirty looks to this day when I see them in public.

Having the whole world gaze at our open wounds, and say "It's all a lie!" and "She made it up to get back at poor Jason!" was incomprehensible. I didn't want anyone to know what happened to Mya. My daughter, son, and I deserved privacy to heal from this overwhelming devastation. Having so many people know what happened, yet not believe it, added additional layers of pain.

None of Jason's friends have the ability to see the truth about him. All they see in Jason is a handsome man who knows how to have fun. Back then, his friends frequently told him he should model, and this went to his head. He constantly bragged to me that he was the best-looking man everywhere he went. People have a tendency to judge others based on appearance, and because Jason was good looking, he was automatically considered a "good" person.

Years of deception, domination, and control over Mya, James, and me gave him the confidence and skill to sweep all his friends under his delusion. Like all psychopaths, Jason is an adept liar, and an expert at making himself look totally innocent and blameless. His words are convincing, and his lies are effortless.

Not one person could see how he manipulated the entire situation from beginning to end.

Rarely will psychopaths admit to crimes. To his friends, I am an outsider. I stayed home taking care of Mya and James every time Jason attended one of their frequent parties. A couple of times, we left our children with a babysitter, and I went with him. Both times, he humiliated me by putting me down in front of his friends, and I never attended another one. Of course, this was intentional to prevent me from raining on his parade again.

The parties he attended were the only places he could be himself. He could get drunk, dance, and have sex with as many women as possible without anyone saying anything, because his friends were doing similar things. Jason's life has always been about the pursuit of pleasure - his selfish, sick pleasure at the expense of others.

After the investigation was over, and Jason fled, I wanted to pack up my kids and move far away. I needed a fresh start someplace else so my kids and I could live in peace, but I didn't have the money to move, especially without child support. Other members of my family lived close by me, and I needed their support physically, mentally, and financially. Moving was out of the question.

The day after I heard Jason left the United States, I made an international phone call to one of his sisters. I told her what Jason had done, and pleaded with her to never leave him alone with her children. She didn't say much, and probably didn't believe me, but I rest satisfied I did my part in warning his family about him. No doubt he has them thoroughly fooled.

A few days after I heard Jason left the country, I contacted his former employer's Human Resources (HR) department to get documents verifying the cancellation date of Mya and James's health insurance. I needed this information to put them on my health coverage policy. The HR department mailed me this information, plus a document naming the beneficiary of his life insurance policy. I expected to see my name there, but it wasn't. Mya's name was there, instead. Not both children's names - just Mya's. What kind of man lists his pre-adolescent daughter as the beneficiary of a life insurance policy?

The pain of finding out I married a child molester who raped his own daughter is indescribable. Nothing else has come close to this pain - absolutely nothing. I think about it every day still, almost 20 years later.

Chapter Eight
Trauma Bonds

Why didn't Mya feel safe enough to tell me or another trusted adult about Jason? Why didn't she understand that the rapes would stop if she told someone? Why did she believe his lies?

I believe Mya was a victim of traumatic bonding, also known as Stockholm syndrome. For the first four years of her life, she developed strong emotional ties with him. She trusted and loved him. She bonded with him. According to RAINN (Rape, Abuse, Incest National Network), if these four situations are present, Stockholm syndrome may develop:

1. Perceived or real threat to one's physical or psychological survival and belief that the abuser will carry out the threat. The abuser may:

   > <u>Assure the victim that only cooperation keeps loved ones safe.</u> (Jason threatened to take her and James far away from me so they'd never see me again, and do something to put me in jail.)

   > Offer subtle threats or stories of revenge to remind the victim that revenge is possible if they leave.

   > <u>Have a history of violence leading the victim to believe they could be a target.</u> (Jason spanked Mya and

James hard, and she knew he wouldn't hesitate to spank her again.)

2. Presence of a small kindness from the abuser to the victim:

In some cases, small gestures such as allowing a bathroom visit or providing food/water are enough to alter the victim's perception of the abuser.

Other times, a birthday card, a gift (usually provided after a period of abuse), or a special treat can be seen as proof that the abuser is not "all bad." (Jason took Mya and James to places geared toward children, gave them candy, ice cream, etc.)

3. Victim's isolation from other perspectives:

Victims have the sense they are always being watched. For their survival they begin to take on the abuser's perspective. This survival technique can become so intense that the victim develops anger toward those trying to help. (I noticed Mya's sadness, and stumbled across a couple of clues that I didn't know were abuse-related. Mya refused to answer my questions, and seemed bothered by my asking.)

In severe cases of Stockholm syndrome the victim may feel the abusive situation is their fault.

4. Perceived or real inability to escape from the situation:

   The victim may have financial obligations, debt, or instability to the point that they <u>cannot survive on their own. (Mya was a child.)</u>

   The abuser may use threats including taking<u> the children</u>, public exposure, suicide, or a <u>life of harassment for the victim.</u> (Jason threatened to take her and James far away from me, so they'd never see me again. She saw no way out of the situation.)

"I have often noticed that the degree of loyalty from a child to an abusive parent seems to be in direct proportion to the seriousness of the abuse the child received. In this counter intuitive way, the stronger or more life-threatening the treatment, the stronger the loyalty from the child."

~David Ziegler

Chapter Nine
Awareness Techniques Fail

"Mya, I know you were afraid to tell me what was happening to you, but I wonder why you never said something to the sexual abuse awareness group that visits your school. They spoke to your class every year. Were you too afraid to tell them, too?"

"Mom, I really wanted to tell them, but I didn't want all my friends to know."

"I don't understand - why would your friends know?"

"Because they said to raise your hand if you're getting a "bad" touch. My whole class was sitting together. I didn't want to raise my hand in front of everybody. I didn't want my friends to know I was getting a bad touch."

Even when asked about receiving a "bad touch," Mya didn't say anything. Fear keeps abused children from disclosing. Fear of her friends finding out and fear of the possible consequences of disclosing abuse prevented Mya from saying anything. When it comes to sexual abuse, parents need to understand that children usually don't disclose, even when asked point-blank.

What a major fail. If professionals can't figure out how to create an environment where an abused child is comfortable disclosing abuse, how can they teach parents the right way to talk to children about abuse? When Mya was in kindergarten, I reviewed "good" touch and "bad" touch on several occasions, and told her to tell Mommy or Daddy if someone gave her a bad touch. She always responded with, "I know, Mom. I know." Speaking to my daughter about "good" and "bad" touches gave me a false assurance that she would tell me if it ever happened. By Kindergarten, Jason had been molesting her for months.

I failed my daughter. The sexual abuse awareness group failed my daughter, too.

If I could go back and do it over, this is what I would say:

"Mya, your body belongs to you. No one has the right to touch you in your private areas. If I give you a bad touch, go tell your teacher or another adult you trust. If Daddy gives you a bad touch, go tell your teacher or another adult you trust. If ANYONE gives you a bad touch, go tell. If your teacher doesn't believe you, go tell another adult you trust. Keep telling adults until someone listens.

People who give bad touches say they will hurt you really bad or do something bad to other people in your family if you tell. Don't believe them. Some adults lie. But don't worry, the police will keep them away from you and the other people in your family. People who give bad touches want children to be afraid and keep quiet. Bad touches won't stop until another adult knows what's going on and stops it."

Sexual abuse awareness groups need to take each child into a room with at least two other adults and ask them INDIVIDUALLY if he/she is getting a bad touch. Even though these programs believe they're making it easy for children to disclose abuse by simply raising a hand, they need to consider that children don't want their peers to know such a horrible secret, a secret they keep hidden under threats from their abuser.

Another reason I didn't consider that sexual abuse was happening in our home is because of how Jason reacted a couple of times when the subject was brought up. We watched a couple of movies on TV about child molestation, and in one of the movies, the abuse happened while the mother was home. The father would punish the children for misbehaving by taking them upstairs, and raping them in the bathroom. The mother could hear her children screaming, "No! I'll be good, I promise!" but she thought he was spanking them. I kept saying, "How could she NOT know?" Jason never had anything to say, he just shrugged his shoulders and shook his head. One time I checked out a library book on child abuse, and showed it to him, tears running down my face. I said, "How any man could look at his own flesh and blood, and rape her, the child he's supposed to be nurturing, and taking care of? What kind of man could lust after a helpless, innocent little child, and damage her mind for the rest of her life?" This time he answered. He said, "A sick one," and walked away.

All the bases were covered - Mya knew about "bad" touches, and knew to tell me if anyone ever gave her one, and Jason told me child molesters were sick. This gave me confidence that child sexual abuse was NOT an issue in my home, and was never even considered. My firm belief that all was well between Jason and the kids was supported by both Mya and Jason's responses.

Chapter Ten
Missed Clues

"The eye sees only what the mind is prepared to comprehend." Henri Bergson

We tend to see the world as *we* are, not as it really is. I didn't look for evil in Jason, especially because he appeared to love his children. It never entered my mind that he was pretending to be a normal father. Jason is an actor, wearing the mask of a good person. Evil usually masquerades as good, otherwise, we'd know to stay away and protect our loved ones and ourselves. I projected my love and concern for Mya and James onto Jason, and believed he felt the same way. Jason was very good at mimicking love and concern for his children in my presence.

As you read the following, please remember, I'm relating this from hindsight. I saw the clues over the space of four years, and never connected them as related. You, the reader, are seeing the clues one right after the other, and they seem obvious as you read them. At the time I saw these clues, they either defied explanation, or I attributed them to having a different causation. To add to the confusion, Jason constantly kept me off guard by engaging me in arguments, gaslighting (a form of psychological abuse that causes a person to doubt his or her sanity, perceptions, and judgment, and causes confusion and anxiety in the victim), put-downs, or blame. He made sure my attention was focused on my "deficiencies" to keep me unaware of what was really going on.

Household clues

Two bent horizontal window blind slats. Folded sheets in the dirty clothes hamper. These inexplicable mysteries occurred repeatedly at home. What did they have in common? In Mya's case, these were signs of sexual abuse.

In my ignorance, I scolded her for bending back the slats, yet I'd find them bent again soon afterwards. I remember feeling exasperated over it, and telling her she was ruining the blinds. She said nothing in response. After Mya disclosed the abuse, this mystery was solved - when Jason raped Mya on her bed, he bent back two of the slats to have a clear view of the driveway so he could know when I got home. Mya told me one time I came home earlier than he expected, and almost caught him.

I remember that day. When I got home, Jason was standing near her closet, which I found a bit odd. She was lying on her bed in her underwear, which wasn't unusual for her, and sobbing. It was a slow, intense sobbing, as if she'd been crying for several minutes. Jason was scowling.

"What happened?" I said.

"I had to spank her for fighting with James." He finished sliding his belt through his belt loops and fastened the belt buckle. Mya and James's petty arguing did get irritating at times, but it was something all siblings did - it certainly was not worthy of a spanking. I didn't want to argue about it in front of Mya - I knew it would set him off and I'd have a huge fight on my hands. At times, his "discipline" was too harsh.

Looking back, I see the scene for what it was. He was hiding his erection from me by facing the closet. And his negative attitude showed me he was already upset and it wouldn't take much for an explosion of anger. I didn't want to start an argument, so I tip-toed around him, like always, and walked into the living room.

The folded sheet mystery was resolved after Jason left our lives. Turns out he placed the sheets underneath Mya while he was raping her, then tossed them in the hamper. He remembered how badly I bled my first time, and he was anticipating the same with Mya. I never suspected folded sheets in the hamper as a sign of abuse.

You may see different signs if your child is being molested at home – try to see things from a different perspective and re-evaluate things that have no explanation, but occur repeatedly.

Request

On a few occasions, Mya requested the "soft" toilet paper. I usually bought the more economical brand, which wasn't known for softness, but for the number of sheets on each roll. I complied when she requested the more expensive toilet paper, because I preferred it, too. I didn't know the reason she requested it was because her genitals had been rubbed raw by Jason.

Red, raw genitals

I saw Mya's genital area red twice. Once when she was four, while I was giving her a bath. I spoke to Jason by phone that night and told him about it. He denied seeing the redness, and I said I'd take her to the doctor the next day if she didn't look better. Of course, healing had begun by the next day, and she was significantly less red.

Another time, when Mya was seven, she called me into her room, and showed me her genital area.

"Mom, look. It hurts!"

"Mya -why are you are so red? Are you using soap when you take a bath?"

"I can't use soap, mom. It hurts too much."

"Baby, you've got to clean yourself or you'll get red and hurt. You need to take better care of your body, Mya. It's important to stay clean." In my ignorance, I blamed my child for the redness.

I told her I would take her to the doctor the following day if she didn't look better. But the next day, there was quite an improvement. Two days later, there was barely a trace of redness. It simply never occurred to me that her own father was rubbing her raw with his penis, and attempting to penetrate her. She was so incredibly tiny, and he knew forcing penetration would tear her flesh.

Twice, I saw stains on her underwear, but I thought she had had a bathroom accident. I didn't want to embarrass her, so I didn't say anything. After the abuse, I realized the source of the stains came from her red, painful genitals. Don't ever assume red genitals are from poor hygiene. Suspect something much, much worse, and talk to your child.

Personality Changes

When Mya was very young, she had a very bubbly personality. She smiled a lot, and was full of wonder, exploring the world with her innocent narrations of "Look, Mommy! Rainbow butterflies!" She was an artistic, sweet soul, with laughter dancing in her eyes. She saw the good and the beauty in the world everywhere. I remember her personality changing, and noticing the light in her eyes dimming. She looked so sad, but every time I asked her what was wrong, she said, "Nothing, Mom." Her smiles and laughter were less and less frequent as she got older. I thought she was picking up the serious personality characteristics of her father and grandmother. But the changes were due to her psychopathic rapist. Jason had stolen her innocence at the tender age of four, and replaced it with fear, mistrust, and sadness.

Some sexually abused children become loners. Look for personality changes – if something is very different about your child, there is a reason.

Sexual aggression

Jason frequently demanded sex as soon as I got home from work and acted desperate to be with me. He couldn't wait until the kids were asleep; he had to have sex immediately. On several occasions, he rubbed me with his penis for a while, and I thought it was strange. Apparently, he was fantasizing about his daughter while rubbing me, then penetrating me. He was reliving his sick pedophile fantasies with me.

A couple of times I noticed red marks covering his stomach as if he had been leaning against something. The marks were actually from Mya attempting to push him away from her with her feet, possibly hands. A few times I noticed that his penis was unusually warm. It was much warmer than the rest of his body because he had been molesting his child.

I recently read that people who connect sexuality and aggression in language or behavior are likely to commit sexual crimes. I had no idea of this when I was married to Jason, but it describes his approach to sex. Besides aggressively grabbing genitals, Jason thought calling me degrading names would turn me on.

Jason and I were in the kitchen when he told me, "You're my whore."

I said, "Excuse me?"

"Yeah. You're my whore. My slut."

Barely able to contain my anger, I said, "Jason, I have only been with you in my entire life. I am not a whore or a slut. You are. You've been with many women. If anyone here is a whore or a slut, it's you. Don't ever call me that again." I rarely said anything intentionally that might get him upset, but that day I spoke my mind.

The connection between aggression, sex, and sexual crimes makes perfect sense. If someone is turned on by using force, coercion, or manipulation of any kind, then children are not safe around them. Sexual aggression toward helpless children is easy for people with this type of mentality.

Observations from others

Jason's past history of cheating led me to suspect he was cheating on me with other women, not molesting his own child. It is rare that a pedophile is attracted only to children; they usually have sexual relationships with adults, too. Child sexual abuse was completely off my radar when it came to Jason; however, two people knew something wasn't right, but I didn't see these warnings for what they were.

The first person to voice her thoughts about sexual abuse to me was Mrs. King, who lived through a nightmare childhood. Her brother raped her for years, and she became pregnant with his baby as a young teen. She opted to have the child, who was sexually abused by Mrs. King's first husband. When she told me these horrible things, I was disgusted, and didn't want to hear any more. I thought she was trashy for having these things happen to her; that the nightmare she lived through didn't happen to normal families like mine. A few weeks later, Mrs. King told me she suspected Mya was being sexually abused by the way Mya played with dolls. I thought she was nuts for saying so, especially given her background. I steered clear of her and her fanciful stories after that.

Mrs. King didn't know that I was so careful - I never let Mya attend sleepovers, she didn't go play at someone's house unless I was there, and she didn't go outside to play unless I was with her, making sure she was safe. No one had the opportunity to abuse her. If she wasn't at school, she was with Jason or me. It was preposterous for anyone to suggest such an awful thing was happening to my child.

The other person to outright say Mya was being molested was an eleven-year-old foster child who lived in our home for four weeks. She was the size of a full-grown woman, and was difficult to control. I remember telling Jason we should ask the foster agency for younger children because it was impossible to get the foster child to behave at times. Jason agreed. I shudder to think what might have happened if another easily-overpowered female child had been left alone with Jason.

Fortunately, Jason was never left alone with the foster child. One evening, I was cooking dinner, and Jason was giving Mya and James a bath. The foster child walked into the bathroom and saw Jason with his hand on six-year-old Mya's genitals. The child was quite upset and called the foster agency. I insisted that Jason was just giving her a bath, not sexually abusing her, and that he would never, ever do such a horrible thing. I was adamant that the foster child's own background of having been sexually abused led her to see sexual abuse where there was none. Jason never said a word. It wasn't necessary, because I defended him so well.

After speaking to the foster agency, I told Jason that Mya was old enough to take a bath by herself. I explained that my father never saw me naked at that age, and that he needed to stop bathing her. Attributing his bathing her at the age of 6 to cultural differences, I excused his behavior.

Longstanding pedophilia

At 21, I was a virgin when Jason and I had sex. I realize now that this is a rare combination. In his mind, I was like a young child due to my innocence. After we were married, he casually told me his ex-wife was a virgin, too, when he got together with her. Seems he was actively seeking out virgin women. Years after our children were born, I was appalled when he told me his ex-girlfriend back in his country was 13 when they were living together. He was 20 at the time. Having sex with underage children seemed to be acceptable behavior in his hometown. When he first moved to the United States, and briefly separated from his previous wife at 22, he dated a 16 year-old girl. He definitely knew it was illegal, because his ex-wife threatened to report him to the authorities. If only she had, maybe he would have been deported and not allowed to return to the United States.

These bits of information, pieced together, show that Jason has been a pedophile for quite some time. I remember seeing him speak to a small group of neighborhood girls, and seeing how he seemed to drink in their faces with his eyes, but I interpreted it to mean that he really loves children. Another time, we visited a friend with young teenage foster children. His face lit up as he gently tossed a softball back and forth with them. It looked so innocent at the time, but I know better now. Every female virgin he sees appeals to him, and he wants to take their innocence, and devour it like the soul-sucking psychopath that he is. His shocking lack of respect for common decency and the law are glaringly obvious looking back at his history. Incest was the next thrilling step in his deviant, disgusting world.

"When people show you who they are, believe them." Maya Angelou

About six or seven years into the marriage, out of the blue, Jason said to me, "You don't really know me."

I said, "What are you talking about? Of course, I know you - you're my husband."

He didn't say anything else. I'm positive he would not have expounded on it, even if I had asked him to tell me more. After all, what man is going to tell his wife that he's raping their daughter?

Another time, toward the end of the marriage, Jason said with a slight smile on his face, "I think I'm a sex addict." I could see he was proud of this new discovery about himself, and having no clue regarding the full extent of his words, I said, "I believe you are." I was going by my experience with him. He couldn't keep his hands off of me, and I was always relieved when he left to go back to work.

Jason told me a few times, "You're book smart, but you don't know anything about real life." He also told me, "You don't live in the real world." He was right. In my world, it was normal to trust one's husband around his own children. In my world, it wasn't necessary to be suspicious of everything one's husband said and did. But I was wrong to live in that world. We live in a world where psychopathic pedophiles exist, and they don't advertise their true characters. They effortlessly blend in with normal people, and be quite difficult to detect. In their minds, people exist to fulfill their sick, twisted desires, or are tools for their pleasure.

Chapter Eleven
Where were you, God?

The first few months after Mya's disclosure left me not only devastated, but numb and in shock. Life didn't seem real. After the numbness wore off, anger set in. How could Jason do something so awful to scar his child for the rest of her life? And more importantly, how could God allow this unspeakable tragedy to happen to an innocent, helpless little girl? Mya told me she prayed for Jesus to make her "daddy" stop giving her a bad touch. Why didn't God stop it? Why didn't God tell me what was happening so I could stop it? Didn't He care that my precious baby was raped?

For a time, I didn't speak much to God, blaming him for allowing it to happen. I continued to go to church with my children, and ignorant people told me everything that happens in our lives is according to God's will, and that He doesn't give us more than we can handle. I couldn't accept that. If God planned for a little child to be raped for years by her own father, He must be a sociopath. There had to be another explanation for why this horrible thing happened to my baby girl.

Years later, I began to understand the principle of freedom a bit better, and learned that God CANNOT interfere with free will - otherwise, where does His control stop? At what point is He supposed to stop a drunken man from plowing his car into another and killing everybody inside? Is God supposed to miraculously cause the drunken man's car to stop just before impact? Or is He supposed to prevent the drunk from getting in his car? Or is God supposed to prevent the drunk from drinking? What about preventing liquor manufacturers from producing alcohol so that no one ever gets drunk? Where should God's control stop? What if we go all the way back to creation, where the first humans were in total and complete harmony with God? God gave them the freedom to choose love or choose selfishness. We see the results of their decision all around us. Only God can heal us from our selfishness, and this healing results from seeing God as He truly is. The sadistic, psychopathic "god" portrayed by much of Christianity has no power to heal minds; it only perpetuates fear and selfishness.

God allows all His creation to have total and complete freedom. Our behavior reveals who we are. The Day of Judgment is simply a diagnosis – we are either healed, and in harmony with God and His principle of other-centered love, or unhealed, and filled with selfishness. God does not control us, and is not to blame for the awful things that happen in our lives. He is not the cause of evil.

Timothy Jennings, M.D., tells a story about one of his patients who experienced sexual abuse as a child, and was having difficulty functioning as an adult because of it. She was angry, especially because her abuser was never punished for his crimes. Dr. Jennings asked her if they could go back in time to when the abuse took place, and everything happened just as it did before, would she switch places with her abuser, or would she rather be the child being abused? She, and 100% of all the other sexually abused patients Dr. Jennings has treated, chose to be the child being abused. They realize there is something fundamentally broken in the mind of a person capable of molesting a child.

A recently published free PDF on one of my favorite Websites beautifully explains how we are all involved in a cosmic conflict, and can be found here:

http://comeandreason.com/files/LTF_StudyGuides/LoveTruthFreedom_StudyGuide_CosmicConflict.pdf

Here's a listing of Websites that have helped me understand why awful things happen to us in the world, and that show God is not to blame:

http://renewedheartministries.com/

http://www.cherilynclough.com/

http://www.godscharacter.com/

http://comeandreason.com/

http://pineknoll.org/

http://gnag.org/

Chapter Twelve
Cruelty all around

"The way a man does one thing is the way he does *everything*." --Zen saying.

I believed it was possible for Jason to be incredibly cruel to me, and yet be kind to his children. Jason was domineering towards me, in every sense of the word. I had grown up with an alcoholic, domineering father, and although he never touched me sexually, I was terrified of him as a child. My father's anger and bad temper ensured he always got his way, and I tried my best to do exactly what I was told, and not incur his wrath. The way my father treated me led me to believe I shouldn't expect to be treated better - not even by my husband. Living with Jason, the same pattern was repeated, and I thought all men are like this. It seemed to be a fact of life. I believed that being married meant I had to endure mistreatment.

It didn't take long for me to find out I was never permitted to deny Jason sex. It didn't matter if I had a fever of 104, severe menstrual pain, extreme morning sickness, or had just come home from the hospital with a painful Cesarean section; how I felt was irrelevant. The only thing that mattered was his desire for sex. Sex is designed to be a source of mutual pleasure for both partners, with each partner giving pleasure to the other, but Jason was all about getting pleasure. He took what he wanted, when he wanted it. Every single day that he was home, he forced me to have sex with him even when I didn't want to. No one can say that he began molesting Mya because he was being denied. He simply wouldn't allow it.

A man who is cruel to his wife is cruel to his children, even if she never sees it. It might not manifest as sexual abuse, but as physical or psychological abuse. When the sexual abuse was disclosed, James felt free to tell me that Jason used to hit him on the head with a belt buckle. I never saw bruises on his head because they were covered by his hair, and James was too afraid to tell me.

My illusions about Jason were based on his outward behavior - he took great pains to make sure I saw him as kind and wonderful to our children. Several times I told him he was a much better father than mine, and that Mya and James were very fortunate to grow up with a father who took an interest in them. He never said anything in response, because he knew the truth about himself.

Jason was a performance whore, an actor, always showing me and others what he wanted us to see. Long ago, he detected my low self-esteem, and knew I didn't expect to be treated well. The illusion of his loving behavior toward his children made me willing to sacrifice my own happiness to ensure my children had what I didn't - a good father. My children needed both parents to grow up stable, confident, and with a strong sense of security. Or so I thought.

It took years, but I learned to forgive myself for being deceived by Jason. My gullibility led to my sweet daughter being tortured for half her life, until I found out and stopped it. Nothing I've ever experienced has hurt more. Besides the death of a loved one, I can think of no greater pain than knowing your little child was raped by someone you both loved. Incest is the ultimate betrayal - for the child, first, and then for the non-offending parent.

Fortunately, with the technology available today, there's no need to rely solely upon your child's response to your questions about "bad touches" at home. It's possible to have definite proof of child molestation taking place, even if your child denies it. Buy inexpensive, tiny, motion-activated spy cameras to hide in a child's room, backpack, and other areas of the house. If possible, buy infrared spy cameras for the bedroom.

Even if you think any noise in the night wakes you up, buy spy cameras for your own bedroom. I know a woman whose husband drugged her when she had migraines, and invited men to rape her while he watched and she slept. One time she woke up during one of the rapes, and saw her husband watching. She had trusted him, never dreaming he would do something so awful. You never know the kind of person you're married to until something like this happens. Child molesters are constantly looking for situations that will allow them to molest, and if you are heavily medicated, anything could happen to your child.

Chapter Thirteen
Nightmares

"Forgive yourself for the blindness that put you in the path of those who betrayed you. Sometimes a good heart doesn't see the bad." --Rob Breszney

For years, the emotional pain of finding out my child was raped by her father was so bad that I wanted to die or be induced into a coma so I wouldn't have to feel anything. I had never known such severe emotional pain could exist - death would have been a welcome relief. But if I died, who would take care of my babies? I had to be strong and raise them to adulthood.

The little snatches of sleep I could get were filled with nightmares. I'd wake up crying, my pillow soaked with my tears. I'd turn my pillow over, and lay in bed for an hour, or more, before drifting off into another nightmare, only to wake up crying again. This repeated all night long for years.

Four nightmares were recurring. In one, I caught Jason in the act of raping Mya. Somehow I had the wherewithal to close the door and grab a huge cast iron skillet from the kitchen. I used the element of surprise to open the door quickly and kill him since I was no match for him strength-wise. In another nightmare, I used a kitchen knife, instead of a skillet. In another nightmare, I had forgotten about the abuse, got back together with Jason, and he continued raping Mya. Again I caught him in the act and killed him. In yet another, I dreamt Mya was 12 years old, and was pregnant with Jason's baby, but refused to say who the father was. Jason suddenly disappeared, and that's when she told me he was the father. It took years for these nightmares to stop recurring every night, in an endless cycle.

Mya, James, and I continued to see Dr. Smith for cognitive behavioral therapy, and I learned breathing techniques to help when feelings of overwhelming despair hit. After a year, we went to an organization specializing in counseling victims of sexual abuse, which included ten months of group sessions.

Though I have not experienced the following methods of therapy, they have been proven to be helpful for severe emotional trauma:

Eye Movement, Desensitization, and Reprocessing (EMDR) - This treatment reduces traumatic memories with the use of eye scanning, sound, and kinesthetic tapping.

Accelerated Resolution Therapy (ART) - ART is a very focused eye movement therapy that works with adults and children. It works quickly, and safely. It has been used to treat anxiety, depression, phobias, relationship issues, grief, and more.

Traumatic Incident Reduction (TIR) - This is a fast method of reducing traumatic stress by re-experiencing it in a safe environment, with no distractions, judgments, or interpretations.

Through therapy, prayer, talking with friends, and time, I processed the trauma. It took years, but thoughts of the abuse stopped consuming my every waking moment. I knew I had finally come to a point of healing when I had a dream unlike any other. It was confirmation that hatred and anger weren't going to destroy me. In my dream, my children were grown, and I was living in an apartment by myself. I heard a knock on my door, and looked through the peephole. It was Jason.

"What do you want, Jason?" I said.

"I need to talk to you. May I come in?"

I opened the door. He looked humbled, broken down, and his clothing was torn and dirty. I pointed at one end of the couch and told him he could sit there, and I sat at the other end. "What do you want to talk about, Jason?"

"I know I've done a lot of bad things to Mya, James, and you, and that nothing can ever erase it."

Several seconds of silence pass, and I say, "You've got that right. Why are you here?"

"I'm sorry for everything I did. I've got nothing - no job, no wife, no home. I miss my kids."

"You're just sorry you got caught, Jason. You would have continued raping Mya as long as you possibly could. Mya and James aren't kids anymore. They're grown up and have children of their own. They don't ever want to see you again. Neither do I." I said this with no anger, no hatred, and no malice. "Come on, I'll buy you a bus ticket to wherever you want and take you to the bus station. But I don't want to hear from you again. Jason, if all the people in the world died except for us, I still wouldn't want anything to do with you. The years I had with you were living hell. The eight years it took for me to recover from living with you were hell magnified a million times. Understand?"

I gave him money for a bus ticket, and dropped him off at the bus station. Then I woke up. After that night, the recurring nightmares stopped. I had worked through years of pain, and relief from the constant nightmares finally arrived.

Chapter Fourteen
Out of the Woodwork

Child sexual abuse stories are everywhere. I kept in touch with one of my former babysitters, Andrea, and found out that she, too, had been molested. And not just by her father, but by his friends and neighbors. Her father treated her like a piece of property, and passed her around for his friends to abuse. Andrea blocked it out for many years, and when she started dating her fiancé, she told him she was a virgin. After they got married, all the memories of abuse came flooding in and devastated her. Andrea's mother had no idea of the abuse, and was destroyed. Andrea was unable to hold down a job because being around men made her so uncomfortable, which is why she babysat. She finally confessed that the reason she abruptly stopped babysitting Mya and James was due to Jason. She told me, "Jason gave me the creeps."

"What do you mean? Did he do something to you?"

"When he came over to get the kids, he'd wear a sleeveless shirt, and flex his muscles. He liked to stare at me and smile. He stood too close - he didn't have any sense of boundaries. I told my husband I didn't ever want to see Jason again, so that's why I quit watching your kids with no notice. Sorry I couldn't tell you why before."

What Andrea didn't know is that *her* husband gave me the creeps. I was shocked to find him babysitting my children one afternoon, when Andrea went out to run a quick errand. Andrea assured me her husband wouldn't do anything to hurt them, and that he was a good husband and father.

A few years after this conversation, Andrea's husband molested their 10 year-old son. The boy immediately told his mother, and she contacted the authorities. Fortunately, Andrea had been diligent in talking to her son about sexual abuse, even telling him that if *she* touched him inappropriately, he needed to tell an adult he trusted. Despite knowing the psychological difficulties his wife experienced due to her own molestation, this psychopathic man still decided to rape his own son.

I was so hesitant to leave my children around any man, and was always suspicious of others. Why did I believe that the man who helped procreate our children was trustworthy? Being related by blood does not prevent a molester from molesting; sharing the same DNA means nothing to some pedophiles.

A year after knowing the truth about Jason, I was surprised to hear another sad story of sexual abuse at my divorce attorney's office. Each semester, I paid my attorney several hundred dollars in person after receiving my financial aid check. One afternoon I went in to make a payment, and his paralegal, Mrs. Jones, looked quite different. She was pale, and appeared shell-shocked.

"Ms. Jones, are you okay?"

"No, I'm not." Tears slide down her face, and she sniffles. "I know what happened to your daughter, because I deal with all the paperwork that comes into this office. Last week I found out my 30-year-old daughter was molested by my ex-husband when she was 10 years old."

My heart broke for her. I know this pain so well. I reach out to hug her. "I'm so sorry."

"He hadn't seen her for years, and spoke to her on the phone one day. He wanted her to visit for two weeks during the summer. I trusted him with her, and put her on a plane to see him. She never told me what he did to her, but said she didn't want to see him again, and I didn't force her to. Now I understand why I had such a difficult time with her during her teenage years. It's all so clear, now."

Painful stories of child sexual abuse are all around us. We must take our heads out of the sand and understand that some of our loved ones are pedophiles or child molesters who jump at the chance to rape helpless children. They have no regard for the pain and suffering of our little ones. Psychopaths relish the power and control they feel over anyone they can dominate. Pedophiles don't care how confusing, painful, or damaging their acts are to another. They do whatever makes THEM feel good, and if our babies get hurt, too bad.

Chapter Fifteen
Rare Stranger Danger

Life is never the same after looking evil in the face, and calling it "husband." It completely changes you to know that someone you trusted, loved, and shared your life with could psychologically torture, rape, and betray his own innocent, helpless little girl. For the rest of my children's childhoods, I couldn't even think about allowing another man into our lives. I truly learned that people who appear selfless and loving could actually be selfish and manipulative. We can only see outward appearances, which are often very deceptive.

Less than 10% of child sexual abuse is from a complete stranger. I don't see every man as a potential child molester, but after being married to one, I'm sensitized to male body language. This sensitivity to body language made me aware of a strange man I'd never seen before in a store four or five years after I found out about Mya's abuse.

Mya, James, and I walked into a big box store to do some shopping. On the left, near the cash registers, I noticed a man looking through a magazine. Just before we passed him, I saw his head move in our direction. I turned around and saw his mouth drop open, and watched his creepy eyes race up and down my son's body two times.

I was livid! I told my kids to stop walking and get behind me, and they complied immediately. With his target hidden, his attention focused on me. I pointed my right index finger at him, and made the meanest face I could possibly make. I must have looked insane, but I know what I saw.

The man closed his mouth, and his eyes opened wide. He stared at me for a couple of seconds, and then looked back down at his magazine. In a voice loud enough for the man to hear, I told my children, "Stay close to me. There's a child molester in this store." We walked away, and I turned around again a few seconds later to see if the creep was watching, but he had vanished. He may or may not have been a child molester, but something was off. A normal man does not repeatedly rove over a child's body with his eyes.

Chapter Sixteen
Present Day

Today, my beautiful Mya has a full-time job, and is married to a man who treats her with love and respect. I am so proud of the woman she is. She not only survived a horrible childhood, she is thriving despite a child molester "father" who attempted to destroy her spiritually, emotionally, and physically. She has a wonderful future ahead of her, and her self-esteem is high.

James is in a long-term relationship with a girl he met at work. He's kind to others, extremely sociable, loves animals, and is still trying to make up his mind about the direction his life should go. He's attending college full-time, and standardized testing indicates he can choose a career in any field.

Questions and/or Comments?

If you like to contact me, send me an email: audreydoomer@gmail.com

Additional Sources of Information about child sexual abuse:

http://www.childmolestationprevention.org/pages/tell_others_the_facts.html

http://www.rainn.org/

http://www.dmoz.org/Society/Issues/Children,_Youth_and_Family/Child_Abuse/Sexual_Abuse/

Before you go...

If you feel this book is valuable, please share your thoughts about it with your friends and family. I'm intentionally keeping the price low because I believe every non-offending parent needs to see how easily child molesters can fool people. If sharing my story helps even one person, then it's been worth reliving the worst years of my life to publish this account.

It's come to my attention that there's an account on goodreads.com filled with negative reviews about this book (former title: "Child Molester: A Shocking True Crime Story of Incest, Deception, and Healing"). I believe the people who wrote these bad reviews are hiding under fake names and photos because they may be pedophiles who want to prevent awareness of pedophilia. Fortunately, there's another account for this book on goodreads.com, and it has positive reviews. If you consider this story helpful, please post a positive review on both goodreads accounts so more people will want to read it and spread awareness of pedophilia, how pedophiles behave, and learn about clues that a child might be experiencing molestation.

Here are both goodreads.com links:

http://goo.gl/vuhjkL

http://goo.gl/SJwQOx

I'd be very thankful if you posted a positive review on Amazon.com, as well.

Here's the amazon link:

http://goo.gl/hgmc9H

Thank you for taking the time to read my story.

--Audrey Doomer

www.ingramcontent.com/pod-product-compliance
Lightning Source LLC
Chambersburg PA
CBHW072250310526
45795CB00011B/676